THE ROUND BOOK

ROUNDS KIDS LOVE TO SING

By Margaret Read MacDonald
and Winifred Jaeger

Illustrated by Yvonne LeBrun Davis

Linnet Books
1999

Text © 1999 Margaret Read MacDonald and Winifred Jaeger.
Illustrations © 1999 Yvonne LeBrun Davis.
First published 1999 as a Linnet Book,
an imprint of The Shoe String Press, Inc.,
2 Linsley Street, North Haven, Connecticut 06473.

ISBN 0-208-02441-7 (cloth: alk. paper)
ISBN 0-208-02472-7 (paper: alk. paper)

The paper in this publication meets the minimum
requirements of American National Standard for
Information Sciences—Permanence of Paper
for Printed Library Materials, ANSI Z39.48—1984. ∞

Designed by Abigail Johnston

Printed in the United States of America

For Alice Rohrer and Rev. Robert Rowland,
the round leaders of my youth.
For Jennifer and Nathanial Whitman, Julie and Tom Martin,
Mary K. Whittington and Winifred Jaeger, and all
the other friends and relatives who helped sing this book into being. MRM

For my sister Marieluise Jaeger
who shares with me the love of singing and who chimed in
to pick some of the best songs for this book. WJ

For my children, Kim, Shannon, Becky, and Seth. YLD

Contents

All rounds can be played on alto and bass recorders (F instruments, reading up an octave). All except those followed by an asterisk* can be played on soprano and tenor recorders (C instruments).

Introduction

Rounds are songs to sing with friends "in the round," over and over if you want to. They are fun to sing because all we have to do is learn one tune. Then, if we divide into groups and begin singing at different points in the song, we end up with a beautifully harmonious sound.

Round singing is a wonderful group activity that can be done by old friends but is also a great ice-breaker for strangers. Many of us don't think of ourselves as natural singers, but this gives everyone an opportunity to participate. It leads as much to laughing as it does to singing, as groups chime in at the wrong time, lose their parts, or (sometimes) all mysteriously wind up singing the same thing at the same time! But practice almost always makes perfect.

This book is divided into thematic sections. Part One, "Sing, Sing Together," contains rounds about the joys of making music together. The rounds in Part Two, "I Love the Flowers," sing the praises of nature. Part Three, "Go to Joan Glover and Tell Her I Love Her," holds playful and flirting songs; and Part Four, "O How Lovely Is the Evening," sings of the approach of night. Then Part Five, "Wake Up!" sings of morning! In Part Six, "Heigh Ho, Anybody Home?", we find songs of friendship. Part

Seven, "Why Shouldn't My Goose Sing as Well as Thy Goose?" contains playful children's songs. Part Eight, "For Health and Strength," is a collection of table graces and songs of praise. In Part Nine, "Now We'll Make the Rafters Ring," we find more complicated rounds for advanced singers, several of which are about round singing itself. In Part Ten, "Rain Turns to Snow," we find rounds for the winter and holiday season. And in Part Eleven, "Sing It Over," we end with four lovely rounds about the joys of music.

Our book follows the path of four young hikers as they set off on a trip, singing as they go. Pacific Northwest artist Yvonne LeBrun Davis has created illustrations showing our four hikers traveling through *The Round Book*. They begin their hike, then stop to pick flowers, play hide-and-seek, sing around the campfire in the evening, are awakened by some animals in the morning, stop to visit friends, play singing games with the children, sing grace over lunch, play a few rounds on their recorders, practice some holiday rounds for the coming winter, and then set off for home.

These rounds are fun for any age. Older youth can master them all easily. For younger children, select lively rounds. "Johnny, Johnny!" (20), for example, can be used with preschoolers if you have two adults to lead the two groups. Brief suggestions on use accompany many rounds. For general advice on using rounds, see "Suggestions for Round Leaders" at the back of this book. Be sure to read "A Brief History of the Round" there as well, to learn something about the interesting background of this musical form. And for those who are hooked on rounds, use the bibliography, "More Rounds for the Avid Singer," to find more excellent collections.

All rounds in this book can be played on alto recorders and on bass recorders (F instruments, reading up an octave). Most can be played also on soprano or tenor recorders (C instruments), except those starred in the table of contents.

Singing rounds is enjoyable around campfires, on hikes, at family gatherings. Some of the sillier ones really draw people together. Some are fun when used as children's games. One of the rounds could enter into your family tradition as a table grace. Some of the hymn-like evening and morning rounds are useful in worship services. In our library programs we use the livelier rounds as story-stretchers to get the young audience up and moving. And we use some of the quieter rounds as crowd soothers, to calm them down.

The round is such a delightful form because it allows inexperienced singers to sound really good. Try it and discover the delights of round singing!

Fun with Rounds

To sing a round you all learn the same tune, then divide into groups and begin singing at different times. When the first group reaches the end of the first phrase, the second group starts singing the beginning of the song. Though each group is singing a different part of the song, because of the muscial form of the tune, the voices blend in harmony and it sounds great!

How to sing a round:

1. To learn the round, begin by singing the tune all together several times until you know it.

2. Look at the music to see in how many parts this round can be sung. Some rounds are two-part rounds, some three, four, or even more. Divide your group into the number of sections you need.

   Choose a leader to start each section singing at the right time and to signal the whole group to stop singing. The music will show where each part should come in.

3. Group one begins singing. After a few bars, group two joins in, then group three. When you are learning the round, watch the music and the leader so you come in at the right place.

4. Listen to each other so that your voices blend. Watch the others in your section so you all stay together.
5. Keep singing the round over and over until the group leader signals. Then get ready to stop.

Rounds are composed so that all singers can end at one time. This gives a harmonious final note and makes a pleasing end. To do this, watch for the leader's signal, then all end when you reach the hold sign ($\frown$) in the line you are singing. Everyone just holds that one note and all end with a lovely chord!

How to make a round sound good:

1. While you are singing, listen carefully to the other voices. Do not sing louder or softer than the others.
2. Keep strict time as you sing a round. If you speed up or lag behind, the parts will not fall together properly and the harmony will be lost.
3. Listen for the harmony from the blending voices as you sing. Try to make your own voice blend with the others.
4. If you keep singing the round over and over, it will begin to sound good.
5. Relax and enjoy yourself!

Singing a round is lots of fun. Thanks to the simple round, we can ALL sing in HARMONY!

PART ONE
Sing, Sing Together

1. Sing, Sing Together

1. Sing, sing to - geth - er, mer-ri-ly, mer-ri-ly sing.

2. Sing, sing to - geth - er, mer-ri-ly, mer-ri-ly sing.

3. Sing, sing, sing, sing!

Singing rounds is a great way to build a feeling of community. All five songs in this section are good starters for a round fest.

2. Come Sing Along with Me

Come sing____ a - long with me
and make____ sweet____ har - mo - ny,
now loud - ly swell - ing, and
now____ soft and low.

This tune invites playing with both group and sound dynamics. Sing LOUDLY on "loudly swelling" and *softly* on "soft and low" for a novel effect.

3. Who Is Happy Is a King

German oral tradition. Translated by Winifred Jaeger

This round reminds us that simple things can bring joy—another good reason to sing rounds! You can try it in German as well:

*Froh zu sein, bedarf man wenig
under wer froh ist, ist ein König.*

4. Let Us Sing Together

Let us sing to-geth - er, let us sing to-geth - er,

one   and   all   a   joy - ous   song,

let   us   sing   to - geth   -   -   er,

one   and   all   a   joy -   ous   song.

Let   us   sing   a   -   gain and   a - gain,

let   us   sing   a   -   gain and   a - gain,

let   us   sing   a - gain and   a - gain,

one   and   all   a   joy - ous song.

Though this round has a longer score than most in this book, you will find it quite easy to sing. The "again and again" clearly shows this tune was meant to go around and around.

5. Viva, Viva la Musica

Michael Praetorius (1571-1621)

"Long live music!" is the sentiment of this round, so clear it needs no translation. Its composer, Praetorius, was so prolific he left us over 1,000 vocal pieces among many other works.

PART TWO

I Love the Flowers

6. I Love the Flowers

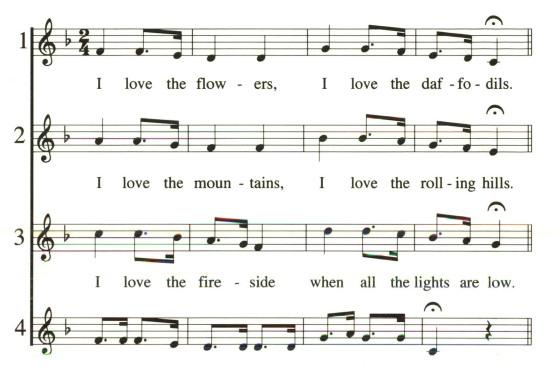

I love the flow - ers, I love the daf - fo - dils.

I love the moun - tains, I love the roll - ing hills.

I love the fire - side when all the lights are low.

Boom - de - ah - da, boom - de - ah - da, boom - de - ah - da, boom!

Here is a great hiking song. The "boom-de-ah-da" keeps everyone in step.

7. Come, Follow Me to the Greenwood Tree

Adapted from John Hilton, 17th century

1. Come, fol - low, fol - low, fol - low, fol - low, fol - low, fol - low me.

2. Whith-er shall I fol - low, fol - low, fol - low, whith -er shall I fol - low, fol - low thee?

3. To the green - wood, to the green - wood, to the green - wood, green - wood tree.

8. To Ope Their Trunks

1   To ope their trunks the trees are nev - er seen.

2   How then do they put on their robes of green?

3   They leave them out!

"Come, Follow Me to the Greenwood Tree" on the facing page is an early round, and involves a call and response. The idea of the greenwood tree turns up in Shakespeare's play, *As You Like It*, with the similar repeated phrase, "come hither, come hither, come hither."

In Round 8 above, a tree "dressing" itself in leaves is the basis for two puns. Can you find them? (Clues: "trunk" and "leave.")

9. My Paddle's Keen and Bright

My pad - dle's keen and bright,

flash - ing with sil - ver,

fol - low the wild goose flight,

dip, dip and swing.

Sometimes campers are inspired to make up new rounds. This canoeing song was composed by Margaret Embers McGee in 1918. After you have sung many rounds and have a feel for this musical form, you might try to compose one yourself.

10. Up and Down This World Goes Round

Matthew Locke (1630-1677)

This seventeenth-century round seems to roll over like a wheel. Notice how the music goes up and down too. There is no fixed ending.

11. They March, They March

You can feel the strong, steady beat in this round. It is fun to lift your knees high and swing your arms as you sing. Try to roll the "r" on the "r-r-rolling drum."

Round 12 opposite, "Laughing Comes the Springtime," turns into a laughing contest. Breathe from your stomach and take good deep breaths so you have plenty of air for all those "ha-has."

12. Laughing Comes the Springtime

1. Laugh - ing, laugh - ing, laugh - ing, laugh - ing
comes the spring - time o'er the_ field,

2. laugh - ing, laugh - ing, ha, ha, ha, ha, ha, ha, ha, ha,
comes the spring - time o'er the field,

3. ha, ha, ha, ha, ha, ha, ha, ha, ha, ha, ha, ha, ha, ha, ha, ha,
ha, ha, ha, ha, ha, ha, ha, ha, ha, ha, ha, ha, ha.

17

13. Grasshoppers Three

Grass - hop - pers three a - fid - dl - ing went,

hey, ho, nev - er be still, they

paid no mon - ey to - ward the rent, but

all day long with their el - bows bent, they

fid - dled a tune called ril - la - by, ril - la - by,

fid - dled a tune called ril - la - by - ril.

14. The Lively Song of the Frogs

In "Grasshoppers Three" on the facing page, it is fun to bend your elbows and pretend to fiddle with the grasshoppers in this tune.

For the frogs in the round above, make your "kriks" frog-like and roll that "r" on the bass frog's "brrr---um!" The tune should sound like a pond full of frogs all croaking at once!

19

15. Laughing May Is Here

20

6 blue - bird____ say:

7 "Mer - ry, mer - ry, mer - ry, mer - ry

8 May!"

Eight parts make this seem a bit more complicated than some, but it has a lovely sound when sung well. The final notes of this song should sound like a bird's cheerful call.

16. White Coral Bells

1
White cor - al bells   up - on a slen - der stalk,
Oh,   don't you wish   that   you could hear them ring!

2
lil - lies of the val - ley deck my gar - den   walk.
That will hap - pen on - ly when the fair - ies   sing.

Sing this flower song slowly and sweetly with bell-like tones. It will have the feel of fairy bells ringing.

PART THREE
Go to Joan Glover and Tell Her I Love Her

17. Go to Joan Glover

Go to Joan Glov - er and

tell her I love her, and

at the light of the moon,

I will come to her.

Imagine teenagers singing this lively courting song in 1609! Composer Thomas Ravenscroft began editing rounds when he was only seventeen—perhaps Joan was someone he admired . . . ?

18. Where Are You Going, My Pretty Maid?

Henry Purcell (1658-1695)

1 Where are you go - ing,

2 my pret - ty maid? I'm

3 go - ing a - milk - ing,

4 Sir,___ she said.

Composer Henry Purcell used this countrified image of the English milk-maid in his round. Purcell invigorated English music in the seventeenth century with his lyrical melodies and his ear for the rhythms of English speech.

19. Where Is John?

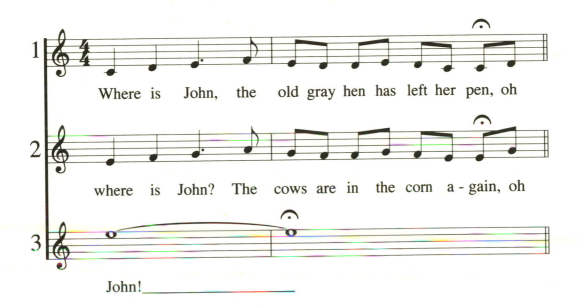

1. Where is John, the old gray hen has left her pen, oh

2. where is John? The cows are in the corn a - gain, oh

3. John!_____

It appears that John has been delinquent in his farm chores. To fetch him, make the most of the call—"Oh John!" Cup your hands to your mouth and call as if you are really seeking that lost boy.

20. Johnny, Johnny!

John - ny,   John - ny!

What?   What?

So   we   keep   sing - ing,   and

so   we   keep   call - ing   him.

This round pairs perfectly with "Where Is John?" on the previous page. Jump from your seat as you sing Johnny's answers, "What? What?" This adds action and silly fun since the group singing line two keeps popping up, calling "What? What?"

21. There Was a Little Girl

Erich Katz (1900-1973)

There was a lit-tle girl who had a lit-tle curl,—

right in the mid-dle of her fore - head;

when she was good, she was ver-y, ver-y good;

when she was bad, she was hor - rid!

Not all composers of rounds lived long ago. Erich Katz used a well-known nursery rhyme in this contemporary round for English school-children.

22. Rose, Rose

This round is a favorite for it is easy to sing and yet creates soothing chords.

PART FOUR
O How Lovely Is the Evening

23. O How Lovely Is the Evening

1 O how love-ly is the eve-ning, is the eve-ning,

2 when the bells are sweet-ly ring-ing, sweet-ly ring-ing,

3 ding, dong, ding, dong, ding, dong.

English church bells clearly inspired this round. Sing it slowly to recreate the clarity of their tones.

24. Rise Up O Flame

Christoph Praetorius (around 1600)

This song can be sung in eight parts or in fewer parts. It is a lovely song, especially for singing around the campfire at night.

25. Tallis Canon

Words by Thomas Ken (1695). Music by Thomas Tallis (1565)

1. All praise to Thee, my God, this night,

2. for all the bles - sings of the light.

3. Keep me, oh keep me, King of Kings,

4. be - neath Thine own al - might - y wings.

This is the earliest round in this book for which we have a date. It is known by the name of its composer, Thomas Tallis, remembered for his hymns, services, and anthems. Its simple tune makes it easy to sing and it has retained its popularity for well over 400 years.

26. Sweet Is the Hour of Twilight Gray

William Hayes (1706-1777)

1. Sweet is the hour of twi - light gray

2. when eve - ning veils the face of day,

3. when shades of night be - gin to fall,

4. the dark - ness soon will cov - er all.

Sing this round sweetly and quietly. It is a good song to sing as dusk falls, or before leaving the campfire.

27. Evening Is Upon Us

Translated by Winifred Jaeger

1. Stay with us, O___ Lord

2. for eve - ning is up - on us,

3. and the day is near - ly end - ed.

This old German round has a quiet hymn-like quality. For those who want to try the original language, here are the lyrics in German:

Herr, bleibe bei uns,
denn es will Abend werden
und der Tag hat sich geneiget.

28. Day Is Done

1 Day   is   done,   gone the   sun

2 from the lake, from the hills, from the   sky.

3 All   is   well,   safe -ly   rest,

4 God is   nigh._____

This tune, known also as "Taps," is played as a finale to events. A lone bugler often plays it at camp as the flag is lowered at day's end. Or it may be heard ringing out in the final moment at a funeral or a memorial service, especially in the military. There is a quality to "Day Is Done" that is both sweet and sad. Sing it thoughtfully.

29. The Cuckoo

In for-ests far a-way we can hear___ the cuck-oo.

From top of his great oak he is call-ing to the owl.

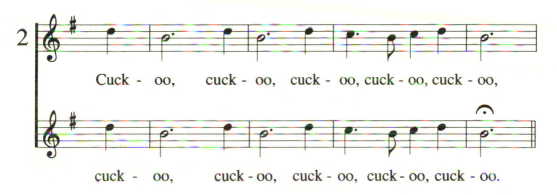

Cuck-oo, cuck-oo, cuck-oo, cuck-oo, cuck-oo,

cuck-oo, cuck-oo, cuck-oo, cuck-oo, cuck-oo.

Make your voices still and clear as you sing your cuckoo's call. Here is the French text for this popular round:

> *Dans la forêt lointaine, on entend le coucou.*
> *Du haut de son gran chêne, il repond au hibou:*
> *Cou-cou, cou-cou, cou-cou, cou-cou, cou-cou,*
> *Cou-cou, cou-cou, cou-cou, cou-cou, cou-cou.*

30. Whippoorwill

1 Gone to bed is the set - ting sun.

2 Night is com - ing and day is done. Whip-poor-

3 will, whip-poor-will has just____ be - gun.

In this round, your voices echo the call of the whippoorwill. The sound of these birds calling all about you in a dark forest is eerie indeed. Their call is exactly like the notes for the word "whippoorwill" in this song.

Reprinted by permission of Girl Scouts of the USA from "Whip-poor-will" by Anne H. Chapin in *The Ditty Bag* compiled by Janet E. Tobitt.

31. Have You Seen the Ghost of John?

No evening around the campfire would be complete without a spooky song or two. Sing this one in the dark, and make sure the "ooo" is a drawn-out wail.

32. Early to Bed and Early to Rise

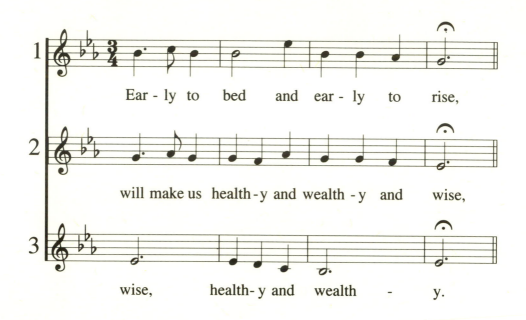

1 Ear - ly to bed and ear - ly to rise,

2 will make us health-y and wealth -y and wise,

3 wise, health-y and wealth - y.

Some rounds use proverbs for their lyrics. Here the words of America's Benjamin Franklin are adapted to an old English round.

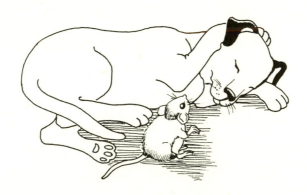

33. Now the Day Is Nearly Done

1 Now the day is near - ly done,

2 night is slow- ly com - ing on.

3 Sweet - ly sleep till morn - ing light:

4 Good - night! Good - night!

Sing this good-night song quietly, and listen to the harmony.

43

34. Good Night to You All

Good   night to you   all,   and   sweet be your   sleep.

May   si-lence sur-round you, your slum-ber be   deep.

Good - night, good - night, good - night,   good - night.

If you sing this as the last song of the evening, it might be good to let each voice finish when it has sung the piece through three times, giving a gentle end to the piece. One group is left alone to quietly finish.

PART FIVE
Wake Up!

35. Wake Up! Wake Up!

Johann Jacob Wachsmann (1791-1853)

1: Wake_ up, wake_ up, the roost - er has crowed,

2: the sun__ steps out on his gold - en road.

Sing the "Wake up" like a rooster crowing and you are guaranteed to have people scrambling out of their sleeping bags! Here it is in German, if you would like to try that:

Wachet auf, wachet auf,
es krähte der Hahn,
die Sonne betritt
ihre goldene Bahn.

36. Are You Sleeping? (Frère Jacques)

Are you sleep-ing, are you sleep-ing,
Frè - re Jac - ques, Frè - re Jac - ques,

Broth - er John, Broth - er John?
dor - mez vous, dor - mez vous?

Morn-ing bells are ring - ing, morn-ing bells are ring - ing,
Son - nez les ma - ti - nes, son - nez les ma - ti - nes,

ding, ding, dong, ding, ding, dong.
din, din, don, din, din, don.

Perhaps along with "Row, Row, Row Your Boat" this is the most popular round known today. Even if you've never heard it, it's a chance to try out some French lyrics!

37. Morning Bells I Love to Hear

Morn - ing   bells   I

love   to   hear,

ring - ing   mer - ri - ly,

loud   and   clear.

Many rounds imitate bells. Think of heavy church bells tolling as you sing this one.

38. Morning Is Come

Morn - ing   is   come,

night   is   a - way,

rise   with   the   sun_____ and___

wel - come   the   day.

This simple round is a surefire success. Sing it early in the morning to draw your group together for the happy day ahead.

39. Merrily, Merrily Greet the Morn

Mer - ri - ly, mer - ri - ly   greet   the   morn,

cheer - i - ly, cheer - i - ly   sound   the   horn,

hark   to the ech - oes,   hear   them   play,   o'er

hill   and   dale   and   far   a - way.

As you sing, your "hark to the echoes" should be clear and loud, like a horn sounding. Listen as each group reaches line 3 and you will hear an echo throughout the round.

40. Sweetly Sings the Donkey

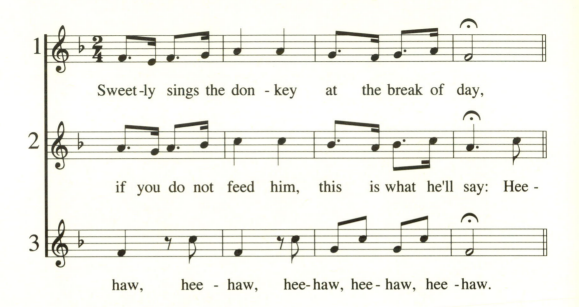

Sweet-ly sings the don - key   at   the break of day,

if you do not feed him, this   is what he'll say: Hee -

haw,   hee - haw,   hee-haw, hee - haw, hee -haw.

Here's a great action song. Throw your hands in the air and toss back your head like a braying donkey each time you sing out "hee-haw."

PART SIX

Heigh Ho, Anybody Home?

Facing page:

"**H**eigh Ho, Anybody Home?" can be sung in three or six parts. To sing this in three parts, the second voice enters when first voice begins line 3; the third voice enters when the first voice begins line 5. It's easy! This cheery refrain is very popular with round singers.

41. Heigh Ho, Anybody Home?

1. Heigh ho,
2. An - y - bod - y home?
3. Meat nor drink nor
4. mon - ey have I none.
5. Still I will be
6. mer - - - - - - - - - - - - - - - ry.____

42. Make New Friends

1. Make new friends, but

2. keep__ the__ old____,

3. one is sil - ver and the

4. oth - er gold.

Another popular round with a useful sentiment.

43. Love Your Neighbor

Love your neigh - bor,

live by la - bor;

would you pros - per,

that's the way.

Some rounds have a moral point, such as this one and "Make New Friends," opposite.

44. Shalom Chaverim

6 L' hit ra - ot,

7 sha - lom,

8 sha - lom.

Here is a lovely Hebrew folk song. Pronounce the ch in "chaverim" as an aspirated h, "ha-vah-rim." Divide your group into as many parts as you can, up to eight, entering the round one line apart. Keep it going around! The words tell your friends to go in peace until you meet again.

45. Laugh, Ha, Ha!

Laugh, ha, ha!

Here's a mer- ry jest,

but if you will laugh last,

you'll laugh best.

Short and easy to sing, this laughing round is based on a quotation from the early sixteenth century which has remained popular through the ages.

PART SEVEN

Why Shouldn't My Goose Sing as Well as Thy Goose?

46. Why Shouldn't My Goose . . . ?

1. Why should-n't my goose

2. sing as well as thy goose

3. when I paid for my goose

4. twice as much as thine?

This is a silly action song. Everyone should leap up as they sing the third, high "goose." It is fun to let each part end alone here, with one final "goose" jumping up at the end. Each group stops singing when it has sung the song through three times.

47. My Dame Has a Lame, Tame Crane

Matthew White (17th century)

My dame has a lame, tame crane,

my dame has a crane that is lame.

Pray, gen - tle Jane, let my dame's lame, tame

crane feed and come home a - gain.

Even the earliest round singers loved to play with words and music. This round is a tongue-twister as well as a nonsense song.

48. Pussy Cat, Pussy Cat

Erich Katz (1900-1973)

1. Pus- sy cat, pus- sy cat, where have you been? I've

2. been in Lon - don to see____ the Queen.

3. Pus -sy cat, pus - sy cat, what did you there? I

4. fright-ened a mouse right un - der her chair!

This old English nursery rhyme was set to music to teach musical principles to schoolchildren. See rounds 21, 53, and 54 for other such rhymes.

65

49. Turtle Slow

1. "Here   I   go,   sure   and   slow,"

2. says   the   tur - tle   down   be - low.

3. "Not so I,   swift -ly fly,"   sings the bird on   high.

You may want to sing the turtle's part very slowly here, but remember that the bird's part must keep to the same rhythm. If the turtle goes too slowly, the bird will sound dreary.

66

50. Donkeys Always Love Their Carrots

1. Don - keys al - ways love their car - rots,

2. car - rots don't like don - keys though.

3. Hee - haw, hee - haw.

4. Cra - zy, but it's al - ways so.

This silly round is from France, but the "hee-haw" works in any language. Try it in French:

> Les ânes aimes les carottes,
> Les carottes n'aimes pas les ânes.
> Hee-haw, hee-haw.
> C'est idiot, mais c'est marrant.

51. Horse to Trot

Horse to trot, to trot,___ I say,

amb-le and amb-le and make no stay,

gal-lop and gal-lop and gal - lop a - way.

Feel the horse's gaits as you sing this, first ambling and then galloping away.

52. Little Tommy Tinker

Lit - tle Tom-my Tink - er   sat   on   a klink - er, and

he   be - gan   to   cry:

"Ma!_____   Ma!_____

What a poor   boy   am   I."

This nursery rhyme is a fun action song. Each group can jump up and throw hands in the air when they reach the "Ma!——Ma!——" part.

53. Little Betty Blue

Erich Katz (1900-1973)

1. Li - tle Bet -ty Blue lost her hol - i - day shoe,

2. what shall lit-tle Bet -ty do?

3. Give her an -oth -er to match the oth-er, and

4. then she will walk up-on two!

Feel the syncopated beat when you sing "hol-i-day shoe" in this nursery rhyme. Can you find the other syncopations?

54. Doctor Foster

Erich Katz (1900-1973)

Doc - tor Fo - ster went to Glo' - ster in a show - er of rain; he stepped in a pud - dle up to his mid - dle, and nev - er went there a - gain.

Enjoy the short, staccato raindrops at the beginning and before you let fall a "shower of rain." Like "Little Betty Blue" opposite, this nursery rhyme was set to music to help children understand music while having fun.

55. How Doth the Little Crocodile

Words by Lewis Carroll. Music by Mary K. Whittington

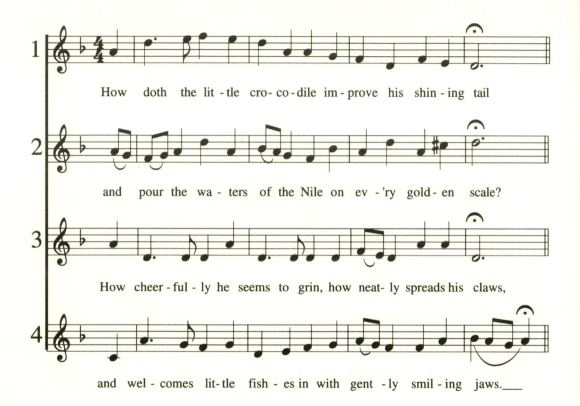

1. How doth the lit-tle cro-co-dile im-prove his shin-ing tail

2. and pour the wa-ters of the Nile on ev-'ry gold-en scale?

3. How cheer-ful-ly he seems to grin, how neat-ly spreads his claws,

4. and wel-comes lit-tle fish-es in with gent-ly smil-ing jaws.___

Here is another round by a contemporary round-lover, using the non-sense poem from *Alice's Adventures in Wonderland*. Alice recites this when she cannot remember the words to "How doth the little busy bee," by the English moralist Isaac Watts.

56. London's Burning

1 Lon-don's burn-ing, Lon-don's burn-ing,

2 fetch the en-gines, fetch the en-gines.

3 Fire! Fire! Fire! Fire!

4 Pour on wa-ter, pour on wa-ter!

You may already know this as "Scotland's Burning," and either way, it's a raucous round! Jump up and wave your arms as you sing "Fire! Fire!" Make the motions of throwing water on the blaze as you sing "Pour on water." This round is historically based. The city of London was destroyed in a great fire that burned for five days in the year 1666.

57. Kookaburra

Koo-ka-bur-ra sits in an old gum tree,____

mer-ry, mer-ry king of the bush is he,____

laugh, koo-ka-bur-ra laugh, koo-ka-bur-ra,

gay your life must be!

The Australian bird, kookaburra, has a call that resembles a laugh. The "old gum tree" in this traditional folk song is a eucalyptus, and "bush" is the Australian term for a certain kind of wild countryside.

PART EIGHT
For Health and Strength

58. For Health and Strength

1 For health and strength

2 and dai - ly bread,

3 we give Thee thanks,

4 O Lord.

This very simple round is a nice grace to sing before meals.

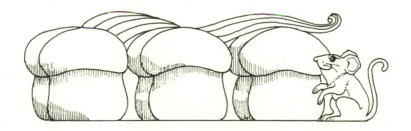

59. O Give Thanks

O give thanks, O give thanks, O give thanks un - to the Lord; He is

gra - cious, His mer - cy en - dur - eth for - ev - er.

This quiet round can be used as a grace or to enhance a religious service.

The round opposite, "Laudate Nomen," is a song of praise in Latin.

In English it translates, "Praise the name of the Lord above all people."

60. Laudate Nomen

Thomas Ravenscroft

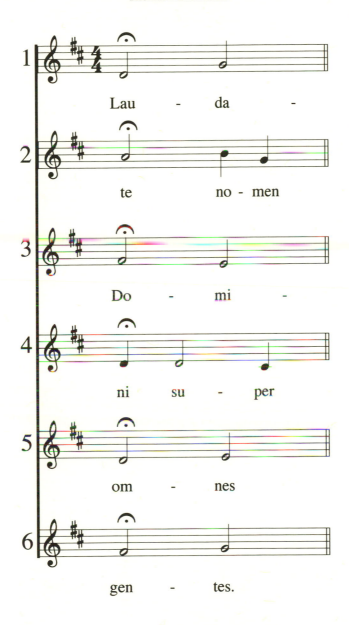

1. Lau - da -

2. te no - men

3. Do - mi -

4. ni su - per

5. om - nes

6. gen - tes.

61. Honor, Praise and Glory

Music by Ludwig Ernst Gebhardi (1787-1862). Translated by Winifred Jaeger

1. Hon - or, praise and glo - ry

2. we of - fer Thee, cre -

3. a - tor of__ all__ worlds,

4. A - men, A - men.

This German round of praise for "the creator of all worlds" can be comfort- ably sung by people of any religious denomination. In German the words are

> *Preis und Lob und Ehre*
> *bringen wir dem*
> *Schöpfer aller Welten!*
> *Amen, Amen.*

"Dona Nobis Pacem" on the opposite page is a liturgical prayer in Latin—the traditional language of the Church of Rome—which was set to music by the Italian composer Palestrina. "Dona nobis pacem" simply means, "Give us peace." This round is widely known and sung.

62. Dona Nobis Pacem

Palestrina (1525-1594)

1 Do - na   no - bis   pa - cem,   pa - cem,
   do - na no - bis pa - - cem,

2 do - na   no - bis   pa - cem,
   do - na   no - bis   pa - - cem,

3 do - na   no - bis   pa - cem,
   do - na   no - bis   pa - - cem.

PART NINE
Now We'll Make the Rafters Ring

63. Now We'll Make the Rafters Ring

Now we'll make the
raft - ers ring,
while__ we__ all this
round will sing.

Here is a simple and satisfying round about singing!

64. Pleasant Is It to Hear

Pleas - ant is it to hear a one-voice mel - o - dy.

But with a sec - ond, the mu - sic sweet - er still will be.

Then with a third voice we join in rich - est har - mo - ny.

Another round about rounds.

65. I Pray, Don't Sing So Loud!

This song is a joke about round singing. Those singing the line about "bawling" should sing LOUDLY, while the others sing sweetly. This round may be about a little contest going on between the groups singing each part, but it also reminds us of an important rule of round singing: We must make our voices blend. No voice should be louder than the others.

66. I'm Not Strong, Sir

1 I'm not strong, Sir, sure, 'tis wrong, Sir,

I'm quite hoarse, Sir, so, of course, Sir,

2 I can't sing a note, Sir, some-thing hurts my throat, Sir,

such high notes my voice do strain;

3 I can-not sing this round a - gain,

tho' I try my best, 'tis all in vain.

67. Let Us Endeavor

Let us en - deav - or to

show that when - ev - er we

join in a song we can

keep time to - geth - er.

Opposite: "I'm Not Strong, Sir" is another joking song about round singing. Perhaps the "Sir" being spoken to is a choral conductor, and the round singer would just like to be excused. Still, high notes and sore throats are a reminder not to stretch our voices too far. Keep on singing this beautiful old English melody, even when the harmonies sound modern. Don't sing this one too slowly!

Round 67 above teaches another important rule of round singing: Keep time together as you sing!

89

68. The Orchestra

1. The vi - o - lin's ring - ing like love - ly__ sing - ing,
the vi - o - lin's ring - ing like love - ly__ song.

2. The clar - i - net, the clar - i - net makes doo-dle doo-dle doo-dle doo-dle det,
the clar - i - net, the clar - i - net makes doo-dle doo-dle doo-dle det.

3. The trump - et is sound - ing ta-ta-ta-ta-ta-ta-ta-ta-ta ta-ta-ta-ta,
the trump - et is sound - ing ta-ta-ta-ta-ta-ta-ta-ta-ta - ta.

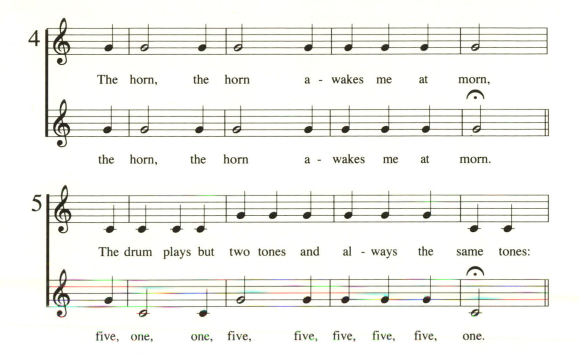

4 The horn, the horn a - wakes me at morn,

the horn, the horn a - wakes me at morn.

5 The drum plays but two tones and al - ways the same tones:

five, one, one, five, five, five, five, five, one.

Enjoy some total craziness with this Austrian folk song. It is fun to pantomime playing the instruments as you sing. This piece can be sung as a round, or each group can take one instrument part and just sing their own part over and over. If you do it this way you might want to sing softly sometimes, loudly others, to avoid total burn-out on your one part. This tune can be sung in a canon form in which each part dies out after it has been sung through a certain number of times.

PART TEN

Rain Turns to Snow

69. Rain Turns to Snow

Winifred Jaeger (1996)

1   Rain   turns   to_____

2   snow___   turns___   to

3   ice   turns   to

In this interesting new round notice how the round itself turns over and over as the rain turns to snow turns to ice turns to. . . . Both the story and the tune are never-ending! Try finishing up when everyone sings an eerie "to."

70. Gone Is Autumn's Kindly Glow

1. Gone is au-tumn's kind-ly glow,

2. now the_ winds of win-ter_ blow.

Many rounds are about springtime, but here is one in a wintry mood.

71. Farewell We Sing

1 Fare - well we sing to man - y hap - py hours,

2 to____ fra - grant walks in sweet and shad - y bow'rs,

3 the win - ter sky a - round us low'rs.

The coming of winter may mean the end of "fragrant walks" but not the end of fun. Singing rounds is a wonderful way to pass the dark winter evenings, especially around a crackling fire.

72. Come Let Us Laugh!

Maurice Green (1694-1755)

Come let us laugh, let us play, let us sing, the

win - ter to us is as good as the spring, the

win - ter to us is as good as the spring. We

care___ not a feath - er for wind or for wea - ther. By

night and by day we sport and___ play, by

night and by day we sport and play, con -

3   fer -ring our___ notes to - geth - er, con -

fer - ring our___ notes to - geth - er,

our   notes, our   notes___ to - geth - er.

And now for a much more difficult round! If you can handle this one you are ready for more advanced round collections. See "More Rounds for the Avid Singer" at the back of this book. There are hundreds of rounds to try!

73. Ring Out the Old

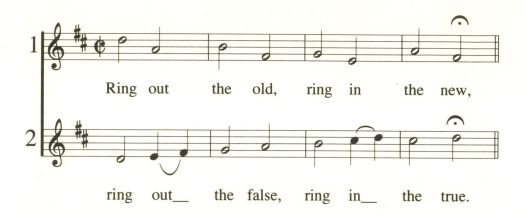

Ring out the old, ring in the new,

ring out__ the false, ring in__ the true.

Here is a lovely round you can use to "sing out" the old on New Year's Eve.

74. Cathedral Bells of France

1. Or - lé - ans, Beau - gen - cy,

2. Nôt - re Dame__ de Clé - ry, Ven -

3. dô - me, Ven - dô - me.

This tune echoes the chimes of the various bells from some of France's cathedrals—Orléans, Beaugency, Nôtre Dame de Cléry, and Vendôme. Sing this slowly and make your voices somber, like deep cathedral bells calling from the highest spires. Hold the final surprise chord as long as you can, getting softer all the time.

75. Grandfather Clock

Karl Karow (1740-1863). Translated by Winifred Jaeger

1. Grand - fa - ther clock is say - ing

tick - tock, tick - tock,

2. mid - dle - sized clock is say - ing

tick - a, tock - a, tick - a, tock - a,

3. ti - ny pock - et watch is say - ing

tick tick tick ticktick tick tick tick tick tickticktick tick.

The trick here is to make the various parts sound exactly like the clocks they name. Grandfather is low and slow. Middle-sized clock is sprightly. And pocket watch is high and light. For added fun, try speaking this round. Enter as you would in singing, but just chant the words and see what happens.

The same tune can be sung as a rainy day round:

Raindrops begin to fall with drip-drop, drip-drop.
Now it is raining faster, drip-drop-drip-drop, drip-drop,
   drip-drop.
Now it 's pouring, run for cover—
Pit-a-pat-a-pit-a-pat-a-pit-a-pat-a-pit.

Or make this into a Christmas song. Give each singer a bell to ring as they sing:

Big cathedral bells are ringing, ding-dong, ding-dong.
Middle-sized bells are singing, ding-dong-ding-dong-
   ding-dong-ding-dong.
Little Christmas bells are ringing, ting-a-ling-a-ting-
   a-ling-a-ting-a-ling-a-ting!

76. Christmas Is Coming

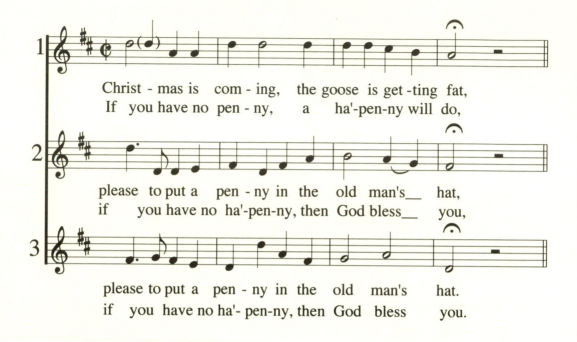

Christ - mas is com - ing,   the goose is get -ting fat,
If you have no pen - ny,   a   ha'-pen-ny will do,

please to put a   pen - ny in the old man's__ hat,
if   you have no ha'-pen-ny, then God bless__   you,

please to put a   pen - ny in the   old   man's   hat.
if you have no ha'- pen-ny, then God bless   you.

This popular song is often used when carolling from house to house. It makes a spirited round.

PART ELEVEN

Sing It Over

77. Sing It Over

Just like rounds 63 through 67, this song is about round singing itself. Its message? Keep practicing until you get it right!

78. In Peace to Dwell

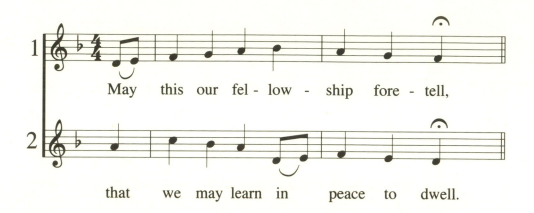

1. May this our fel - low - ship fore - tell,

2. that we may learn in peace to dwell.

A very sweet round on a very important subject. Sing it to build harmony in your group, both musically and socially.

79. A Merry, Laughing Round

1 A round! A round! A mer-ry, laugh-ing round,

2 a mer-ry, laugh-ing, mer-ry, laugh-ing round we sing.

3 A round! _____

A spirited round of laughter that gets better as it speeds up. Be sure to take a good breath on the last line so you can hold the final "round" for four measures.

80. Music Alone Shall Live

1. All things shall per - ish from un - der the sky,

2. mu - sic a - lone shall live, mu - sic a - lone shall live,

3. mu - sic a - lone shall live, nev - er to die.

This joyous final song in praise of music is popular in many countries. Here is how it is sung in Spanish:

> *Todo en la vida perecerá.*
> *Pero la música, pero la música,*
> *Pero la música, no morirá.*

and in German:

> *Himmel und Erde müssen vergehn,*
> *aber die Musici, aber die Musici,*
> *aber die Musici, bleiben bestehn.*

A Brief History of the Round

No one knows just how long rounds have been sung. The earliest round found is a piece called "Sumer Is Icumen In" ("Summer Is Coming In"). It was once thought to have been written down around the year 1227, but nowadays scholars think that happened in the following century.

Rounds seem to have been popular in England at the time of Shakespeare, in the early seventeenth century. He mentions round singing in several of his plays, and even has characters singing a few. Between 1609 and 1611, the young English composer Thomas Ravenscroft edited three sizable collections of music, much of it of anonymous authorship, containing numerous rounds—including "Three Blind Mice." In 1612, David Melville of Scotland published a hefty collection. Although the two had never met, their collections contained many of the same rounds, so it seems that rounds were popular enough to have spread widely. German, Italian, and French composers had taken to the round form, too, and were composing pieces of their own around this time.

By the end of the century, "catch clubs" had become popular in England. The members of these all-male clubs loved to make up new rounds, and the clubs published volumes of these often bawdy works.

Also known as "circle canons," rounds are such a satisfying form of music that musicians, including many well-known composers, have continued to write them up to the present.

Rounds can be simple, complicated, devotional, political, funny. The form of a round seems natural to people because we use imitation in our lives every day, such as copying each other and taking turns. This art form gives us a good feeling, sharing words while making music—someone singing ahead of us, someone following, or both. Round writing takes skill, as each part must sound in harmony with each of the other parts at all times. Nonetheless, another reason why rounds are still widely loved is that they offer an easy way to create harmony.

This book includes rounds written in each century from the sixteenth to the twentieth, many of them from the folk tradition. If you love round singing and are eager for even more rounds to try, check "More Rounds for the Avid Singer" at the back of this book.

Suggestions for Round Leaders

Many of the melodies in this book are enjoyable enough to sing just as songs, in unison. Leaders may want to begin singing rounds with easy two-part pieces, such as rounds 73 and 78. Easy three-part rounds such as 1, 11, 19, 23, 34, and 80 are no more difficult to lead because the richer harmony will delight everyone in the group and help the singers find their places. Among four-part rounds, some of the easier ones are 17, 36, 38, 43, 58, and 67.

You will need to start each section singing at the right time. When is the right time? Look to the left of the music staff. The numbers there are your cue. When the first group reaches the number 2, then the second group chimes in at the beginning of the round. When the first group reaches the number 3, then the third group starts at the beginning . . . and so on.

As a round leader, everyone must be able to see you. When you want the singers to end on the next hold (⌢), raise an arm to signal. Keep your arm up to make everyone stay on that note until all are holding. Then give a different signal to stop together, such as a strong nod or a hand motion.

Every round sounds best when all parts have joined in and are singing together. But quite a few rounds of five or more parts can be successfully sung with fewer voices than the total number of lines. Don't wait to have eight people who can each hold a part before you sing "Shalom Chaverim" (44) as a round! Be adventurous. Experiment until you find the combination you and your group like best.

Let someone who knows a song demonstrate several times how it goes before you try singing. Keep listening. Often an instrument can help you pick out the notes—a piano, recorder, flute, accordion, or whatever. Sometimes it is enjoyable to mix instruments and human voices, but rounds are first of all songs, with words that shape what the music does.

The music here does not show how slow or fast the pieces are to be sung, or how loud. Fast is not more desirable than slow if it does not fit the words or the melody of a particular song. Use imagination in choosing the right tempo for your group. Decide when it is appropriate to sing gently and when to test the vocal cords.

Rounds provide good material for learning to sight-sing and to read music. To use the rounds in this way, watch the size of the steps the melody takes as it moves up or down. Notice when it stays on the same note. Pay attention to how long and short notes are written.

Upon beginning a round, if you do not know the best pitch, take a guess and begin on a random note. You will soon find out whether you need to start the piece higher or lower. The pitches chosen for this book are suitable for most singers, especially for young voices. If a different pitch is more comfortable for your group, there is no reason not to make a change. Sometimes it is necessary to compromise between people who cannot sing very high or very low.

When children, women, and men are singing together, try to end your rounds when the lowest voice—usually a man's—is on the lowest note under the hold sign. This creates the proper harmony and an especially pleasing chord.

There is an alternative way of ending rounds when you want a quiet ending ("Good Night to You All," 34), a special effect ("Why Shouldn't My Goose . . . ," 46), an instrumental solo ("The Orchestra," 68). Try this and see which way you like best. Ignore all hold marks. Let the singers begin as usual, singing in parts from the beginning to the end of the song—for example, three times—and then let each part stop singing at the end of the last line. The parts die out one at a time, just as they started one at a time.

So sing rounds any way you want. They will provide you with a portable pleasure which can be sung wherever you go. Since rounds need no instrumental accompaniment, they are great for hiking, campfires, long car rides. If you sing the rounds in this book many times you will remember them when you need them. Then on that next summer vacation or winter retreat, you can teach them to your friends and make great music together!

More Rounds for the Avid Singer

Anderson, Ruth. *Rounds from Many Countries*. New York: G. Schirmer, 1961. A collection of fifty canons for singing and recorder playing.

Delmar, Gloria T. *Rounds Re-Sounding*. Jefferson, N.C.: McFarland, 1987. A hefty collection with a good historical introduction and rounds from many periods.

Ellinwood, Robert, ed. *Hiking a Round: Musical Rounds for the Outdoors*. Seattle,WA: The Mountaineers, 1996. A useful collection of rounds with a demo tape for some.

Finckel, Edwin A. *Now We'll Make the Rafters Ring*. Chicago: A Capella Books, 1993. Some traditional rounds, some written by Finckel.

Langstaff, John. *Sweetly Sings the Donkey*. New York: Atheneum, 1976. Brief illustrated children's collection.

Nelson, Esther L. *The Great Rounds Song Book*. New York: Sterling, 1985. Children's collection.

Rounds for Children. New York: Amsco Publications, 1986. Children's songs in paperback.

Taylor, Mary C. *Round & Round*. New York: William Sloane, 1946. A very full collection, including many early rounds and an historical introduction.

Taylor, Mary Catherine and Carol Dyk. *The Book of Rounds*. New York: E.P. Dutton, 1977. Includes a good historical essay.

Terri, Salli. *Rounds for Everyone from Everywhere*. New York: G. Schirmer, 1961. Interesting collection, including several from other cultures.

There Were Three Ravens: Songs, Rounds, and Catches by Thomas Ravenscroft. Performed by The Consort of Musicke. CD. Virgin Classics Ltd., 1991. Liner notes are included with the words.

Title/First Line Index

All rounds can be played on alto and bass recorders (F instruments, reading up an octave). All except those followed by an asterisk* can be played on soprano and tenor recorders (C instruments).

But though be little to bee gotten by them,
yet pittie were it, such Mirth should be forgotten of us.

—Thomas Ravenscroft, 1609